My Family Band

Written by Ben Farrell
Illustrated by Karen Strelecki

HARCOURT BRACE & COMPANY

Orlando   Atlanta   Austin   Boston   San Francisco   Chicago   Dallas   New York
Toronto   London

Grandpa will be there with his piano.

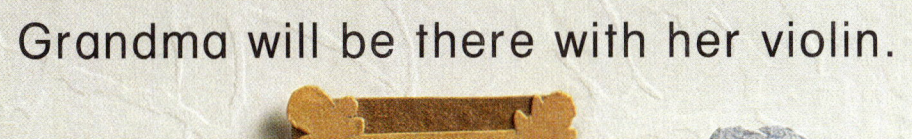

Grandma will be there with her violin.

Father will be there with his guitar.

Mother will be there with her tuba.

Uncle will be there with his horn.

I will be there with my drum.

Everybody will be there—
playing, singing, and dancing!